MEN OF THE SPIRIT

Men of the Spirit

HOWARD LEWIS
AND
DAVE ROBERTS

KINGSWAY PUBLICATIONS
EASTBOURNE

First published 2002

ISBN 1 84291 106 6

Published by
KINGSWAY COMMUNICATIONS LTD
Lottbridge Drove, Eastbourne BN23 6NT, England.
Email: books@kingsway.co.uk

Book design and production for the publishers by
Bookprint Creative Services, P.O. Box 827, BN21 3YJ, England.
Printed in Great Britain.

Contents

Preface

We trust that this short book will stimulate and encourage you. It can be used in two ways. You can read it for yourself, or you can use it as preparation for small group discussion with a group of men.

At the end of each chapter is a structured outline for group work. Here's the thinking behind each of the different parts of the study.

Discuss

This seeks to ask questions that will draw out stories from the everyday lives of the men in the group. It helps them to ground the subject to be discussed in the realities of their lives.

Reflect

This section guides men towards the wisdom of the Bible and its application to daily life. It may refer to a scripture or ask men to suggest relevant scriptures.

Instruct

This points to specific texts and principles that will aid discipleship.

Pray

This includes suggestions for prayer and helps root the discussion in the reality of our relationship with God.

The structure allows for both purpose and flexibility. Men are often more engaged by discussion than passive listening.

If you are new to small group work you might find the Appendix helpful – it's short and practical.

May God give you wisdom and encouragement as you read on.

Dave Roberts

Introduction

Our plans had not included a trip on the ring road, let alone spending most of that Friday evening driving round and round it. It was not where we wanted or needed to be, but the speed, density and aggression of the Parisian traffic had forced us onto it. The choice had been stark: go with the flow of traffic or perish. With most of our holiday ahead of us, we decided it was too soon to perish, so we went with the flow!

But even worse than finding ourselves on a road we didn't want to be on, was the gradual realisation that we were totally incapable of finding any road that would bring us back to the route we actually needed! We travelled round the ring road several times before eventually being rescued by some observant French police officers who had seen the same little red car pass them on numerous occasions. Believing that there were other parts of the city we tourists ought to see, they stepped out of their patrol car and waited for us to complete our next circuit. As we approached them they signalled to us to stop and, after a brief conversation at the roadside, led us with remarkable ease to the escape route we had been searching for.

A casual observer that evening would have seen our car and assumed, wrongly, that we knew where we were going and that we were actually going there. A closer analysis of the scene, however, would have revealed that we really had no idea where we were, and still less idea of how to go anywhere else! While the wheels were turning, we were, to all intents and purposes, going nowhere. There was much activity but absolutely no accomplishment. We were simply going round in circles.

That incident has stayed fresh in my mind over the years. As well as a constant reminder to me not to dice with death by driving within a hundred miles of Paris, it is a vivid illustration of the spiritual struggle that I, and I suspect many other men, face on a daily basis: the struggle against ineffectual Christian living and the struggle to experience Christian growth and maturity. Paul wrote to the Ephesians that the ultimate goal of the believer is to 'become mature, attaining to the whole measure of the fulness of Christ' (Ephesians 4:13).

As a Christian I am active. My life is busy, and that busyness is the expression of a genuine desire to serve Jesus Christ with all my time, resources, talents and energy. But active as I am, I am not convinced that I am accomplishing very much of real significance. *Spiritually I seem to be going round in circles rather than moving forwards.*

As a Christian I am religious. I engage in all the right religious practices, I am committed to all the right religious principles and I am mixing with all the right religious people. But religious as I am, I wonder sometimes whether religion has taken the place of a genuine relationship with God. *Spiritually I seem to be going round in circles rather than moving forwards.*

As a Christian I have a story to tell. The greatest story any man can ever have or tell. It is the story of how, as a sinner, I have been reconciled to God by the death of his Son. It is the story of grace, and I, like every Christian, have been commissioned to share that story with others: 'He has committed to us the message of reconciliation. We are therefore Christ's ambassadors, as though God were making his appeal through us' (2 Corinthians 5:19–20). Yet despite having this story and the commission to tell it, I find that I am more often secretive than sharing. *Spiritually I seem to be going round in circles rather than moving forwards.*

As a Christian I delight in the songs of sacrifice: 'Take my life and let it be, consecrated, Lord, to Thee.' But all too often I sense that they are simply songs, fine words and pleasant tunes – totally unreal in terms of reflecting a willingness on my part to take up my cross and follow Jesus. I love comfort and I lack commitment. *Spiritually I seem to be going round in circles rather than moving forwards.*

Jesus understood well the potential tragedy of his followers being ineffectual in their Christian experience, while being active, religious, converted and comfortable. And in his very last words on earth, recorded in Acts 1, he dealt with just that issue in the simplest but strongest of terms. He left his disciples in no doubt that the key to living a life of growth, progress and maturity is a willingness to respond to the prompting and power of the Spirit of God. Only when we become 'men of the Spirit', not only in name but in reality, can we acquire the transforming power that will enable us to move from activity to accomplishment, from religion to relationship, from secrecy to sharing and from comfort to commitment. Men of the Spirit are men of maturity.

In the following chapters we will examine what it means to be men of the Spirit. It is my prayer that as we think about the subject, and work through the study material, we will not only warm to the idea of rejecting ineffectual Christian living, but we will rise to the challenge of allowing the Spirit of God to energise us and enable us to 'become mature, attaining to the whole measure of the fulness of Christ'.

I for one have spent too much time on a spiritual ring road, going nowhere. The time has come for progress. The time has come for maturity.

Howard Lewis

1

Waiting in Jerusalem

Men of the Spirit move from activity
to accomplishment.

'Do not leave Jerusalem, but wait . . .' (Acts 1:4)

'Wait!' I can think of very few words in the English language that
frustrate me more. In my experience, waiting has never been easy.

Waiting is not easy because it challenges my impatience. I am
a 'now' person, someone who will always opt for instant coffee
rather than wait for the slow process of percolating to come to
an end, even though I know that if I do wait, the final product
may well taste much better. As I write these words I am in a hos-
pital ward, enormously frustrated because I have to wait: I have
to wait for the consultant to do his ward round; I have to wait for
the scanning machine operatives to have a vacant slot in their
timetable when they can fit me in; I have to wait for the results
from yesterday's tests to arrive back at the ward. All around me
are doctors and nurses who seem to think that there is no great
hurry; that if things don't happen today then tomorrow will suit
just as well. Don't they understand that I want action and that I
want it now?

Waiting is not easy because it challenges my activist spirit. It
stops me in my tracks when I don't want to stop. I am the first to
stand when the aeroplane engines are switched off, even though
I know that the other passengers will block my progress to the
exit. I am the one who rushes to the luggage carousel, even
though I am aware from experience that there is a long wait
ahead of me before the eventual arrival of my case. I am the one
who sits at the traffic lights with my foot on the clutch, revving
the engine like a Grand Prix driver, ready to leap forward the very

13

moment the red and amber lights give off the faintest of glows. I am the one who jumps from queue to queue at the supermarket checkout, determined to reduce my waiting time by every possible second. I am an activist. I need to be doing. And I need to be doing now. Waiting is not an option I even want to consider.

Waiting is not easy because it challenges my pride. It forces me to admit to and express a humbling dependence on someone else. There is not a task around my house that I have not enthusiastically attempted at some stage. Plumbing and plastering, decorating and demolishing, wallpapering and wiring are all tasks I have undertaken with enthusiasm and confidence, because my pride tells me that I can do it. Unfortunately all my attempts at DIY stand in united witness to the fact that enthusiasm is an unreliable measure with which to gauge effectiveness and skill, and there are countless delighted tradesmen in my community whose appointment books have been filled and bank balances enlarged as they have been called in to undo the consequences of my enthusiastic but totally inept efforts.

Yet I never learn. I still prefer to attempt things myself rather than wait for the expert to have time to help, because waiting hurts. It is the confession of failure, the acknowledgement that the task before me is a task beyond me, and that I lack the resources to take it on. Like so many men, I suspect, I find such acknowledgement a bitter pill to swallow. In my experience, with the single exception of admitting to being bad golfers, few of us ever admit readily to failure in any area of our life. Even in my most honest moments, I hesitate to admit that I am a poor husband, a poor father, a poor worker, a poor preacher, a poor driver.

But Jesus says to his early disciples and to me, 'Wait.' Despite the pain of having your impatience, activist spirit and pride challenged, wait. Wait in Jerusalem.

Why is it necessary to wait? Is enthusiasm not enough? The disciples had enthusiasm beyond measure. First, they had enthusiasm for their message. The message of the cross had left them downcast, disappointed and disillusioned. Their dreams were shattered. But now they had heard a radically different message from a death-defeating, resurrected Jesus, and they were excited by it. They had heard the message that Jesus was alive, that the grave had been unable to hold him, that Satan had been defeated, that sin had been conquered, that salvation had been achieved, that heaven had been opened. This message had transformed their own lives over the previous few weeks and they were enthusiastic about it as they realised its potential to transform the lives of others also.

> After his suffering, he showed himself to these men and gave many convincing proofs that he was alive. He appeared to them over a period of forty days and spoke about the kingdom of God. (Acts 1:3)

Second, they had enthusiasm for their task. They realised that the responsibility to take this message out into the world was theirs, and they had such a profound awareness of the transforming power of the gospel that they could hardly wait for the opportunity to go out and share the message with the world.

Their enthusiasm was undeniable, and their enthusiasm was good. It is always sad to find those who, for one reason or another, have lost that delightful, infectious, innocent characteristic of being childlike in their excitement. The disciples weren't guilty of losing that. On the contrary, they became more enthusiastic by the hour, straining to get on with the work of telling the world about Jesus.

It was to such an enthusiastic group that Jesus appeared on that last day with the word they desperately needed to hear but definitely didn't want to hear – the word 'wait'. Why? Because Jesus knew what they and I and perhaps so many others so easily forget: the fact that while enthusiasm is to be applauded and encouraged, enthusiasm does not equal effectiveness. If these disciples were to be effective in building God's kingdom on earth, they needed more than enthusiasm. They needed power. And for that power they needed the presence of the Spirit of the living God, and for that presence they needed to wait.

Waiting in Jerusalem is in effect saying, 'I am a poor follower of Jesus Christ. I have a task to perform and while I have enthusiasm for that task, I am incapable of doing it. All my experience, expertise, skills and inner resources count for nothing. I need help.' Everything within me fights against such an admission – all my impatience, all my activist inclinations, all my pride, which wants everyone to believe that I am capable of accomplishing any and every task I am given. And not only everything within me, but the enemy outside me also whispers constantly in my ear that I do not need to wait. Satan is more than happy for me to engage in Christian work, as long as I do it in my own resources rather than in those that become mine as I wait for spiritual power. He knows that nothing but failure and ineffectiveness lie ahead if I fail to wait, and that all my activities will pose no threat to his kingdom.

Sometime before the events recorded in Acts 1, Jesus had explained to his disciples that when it came to evangelism or any other area of Christian service, they were going to be totally dependent upon him. Effectiveness, he had taught them, would come not from experience but from dependence: 'I am the vine; you are the branches. If a man remains in me and I in him, he will bear much fruit; apart from me you can do nothing' (John 15:5).

A few years ago I was taken round a vineyard in the former Soviet state of Moldova, just before the harvest time, when the grapes would be picked and pressed. The scene before me was a picture of incredible life and vitality. The branches were almost breaking under the strain of the massive bunches of grapes hanging from them. Yet there were a few branches that were totally barren. They were branches from the same vines in the same vineyard, existing under the same climatic conditions. They were identical in almost every respect to the fruit-bearing branches, but they were barren, empty, useless and pitiful. The only difference between the two was that at some stage during the previous few months, these now barren branches had been broken off the vine and were lying withered on the ground. It was a perfect illustration of the truth of Jesus' words. Fruit grows, not because of any inherent strength within the branches, but because of the power, energy and life-giving force of the vine, and those branches that maintained the graft onto the vine were able to carry the fruit the vine produced, while separated branches became immediately barren. Jesus is very definite on the issue. Without him, without a vital, dynamic, energising graft onto him, we can do nothing. It is not even worth our while trying to exercise a ministry for the kingdom of God. The essential starting place for service and effectiveness is learning to wait. 'Do not leave Jerusalem, but wait.'

Waiting is difficult. But waiting is possible and the disciples proved that. How can we today rise above the compelling pressures of impatience, activism and pride, and learn on a daily basis to be dependent people, to say 'no' to the inner and sometimes outer suggestions that we are at a point of spiritual maturity and expertise that enables us to function effectively without the daily infusion of the power that comes from waiting for the re-energising Spirit of God?

There are three things that stand out about those first disciples as they temporarily set their enthusiasm to one side and settled down to wait. First, they believed the promises of Jesus: 'Wait for the gift my Father promised, which you have heard me speak about. For John baptised with water, but in a few days you will be baptised with the Holy Spirit' (Acts 1:4–5). When Jesus told them that they needed to wait and that the wait would be worthwhile, they believed him implicitly. There was no debate or discussion about the truth and reliability of his words. They accepted without question that what he said was the truth.

We need that same childlike acceptance of the reality of Christ's claim to be 'the way and the truth and the life' (John 14:6). When Satan first burst upon the scene of human history it was with the claim that God was a liar. God had said to Adam that the consequences of disobedience were that 'you will surely die' (Genesis 2:17). Satan declared, 'You will not surely die' (Genesis 3:4). Ever since that first encounter, Satan has suggested to mankind that God's word is unreliable and it is to be doubted and denied. Even as Christian men we are exposed to the very real temptation to question the truth of Scripture, if not in terms of mental belief then at least in practical terms. So when we hear Jesus saying to us 'Apart from me you can do nothing' or 'Wait for the gift my Father promised', we find ourselves reacting in self-confident assurance that we can do a great deal and we do not need to wait. The disciples rose above and resisted that temptation. They believed the promises of Jesus, and it helped them to wait.

Second, the disciples waited because they understood the significance of their task. Immediately after Jesus had left them, they were met by two angels who spoke to them of the future: 'This same Jesus, who has been taken from you into heaven, will come back in the same way you have seen him go into heaven' (Acts 1:11). The vision was clear. Jesus was going to return to bring all things to a mighty, glorious conclusion, but before that could happen his gospel had to be proclaimed, his grace had to be preached, his kingdom had to be built and his people had to be saved. This was no small, unimportant, trivial task that they were about to take on; it had enormous consequences. It was about eternal realities; it was about life and death, eternal life and eternal death; it was about heaven and hell, about light and darkness. Hearing the message of the angels, the disciples understood the significance of their task, and in that understanding they realised the tragic consequences of failure. The stakes were too high for them to run the risk of working without waiting.

Perhaps for many of us the time has come for a radical reassessment of the significance of our Christian service. Perhaps we have become so used to preaching, to teaching, to leading worship, to serving others in Christ's name that we have lost sight of what is really happening. We have forgotten that through our service God is building his kingdom in preparation for the most glorious day in human history since the day of its beginning; the day when 'at the name of Jesus every knee should bow, in heaven and on earth and under the earth, and every tongue confess that Jesus Christ is Lord, to the glory of God the Father' (Philippians 2:10–11). We need to recapture such a vision for the future and such a dread of failure, that we are driven afresh on a daily basis to a dependent waiting for power. The disciples had it, and it helped them to wait.

Third, the disciples waited because they were supported in doing so by one another. They believed in fellowship. 'When the day of Pentecost came, they were all together in one place' (Acts 2:1). Told to wait, and realising the frustration of a delay before they could take on the task to which they were enthusiastically committed, they saw the need to remain together, a united, coherent group, there to support one another and to exercise mutual restraint when the temptation to go out in their own energy was strong.

One of the biggest weaknesses we face, especially as men, is our failure to recognise or to confess our need of one another, to encourage and support one another in our Christian living. We find it hard to wait because we try to wait alone.

Team means everything. Back in 1988 I was involved in the establishment of two charities. As well as beginning in the same year, they had other things in common. They were both Christian charities, they were both set up to minister to real needs around the world, and they were both spearheaded by passionate, compassionate and enthusiastic Christian men. Yet today there is a dramatic difference between the two. One has an annual income of many hundreds of thousands of pounds and is accomplishing incredible things around the world, while the other has an annual income of only a few hundred pounds. What makes the difference? It is not vision, nor enthusiasm; it is not the ability to communicate the message of the work. What makes the difference is others. One has developed a team to work with and for one another; the other remains under the sole control of an isolationist. I am convinced that so much of our impatience, activism and pride, which propels us into action when we should in fact be waiting, would be much more easily and readily subdued if we were to submit ourselves to the discipline and restraining power of a group within which we share our weaknesses and struggles. The disciples kept together, and it helped them to wait.

For impatient, active, proud people to wait is an incredibly difficult call to receive, and a dreadfully painful word to hear, but even so it is an achievable and worthwhile exercise. For the first disciples, strengthened for the waiting process by belief, vision and fellowship, they discovered that waiting transformed certain failure into certain victory. And for us today as well, waiting in Jerusalem is the fundamental requirement if we are to be people who have abandoned stationary Christian living and who are moving towards maturity; people who at the end of the journey of life will be able to look back, not merely on an active life, but a life of accomplishment also.

SMALL GROUP STUDY

Discuss

What's the longest you've ever had to wait for something? How did you cope? Was it worth the wait?

Reflect

Have you ever done a job (at work, home or church) where you wished you knew more before you started? Describe the situation.

Instruct

The disciples waited in Jerusalem for the gift of the Spirit. What does the Spirit give to those he indwells? The answer is threefold:

Godly character

Read Galatians 5:22–24. Ask your group to consider why this would have been important for the disciples (Peter and his anger in Gethsemane; disciples sending away children; brothers bickering over position in heaven, to name but three).

Godly insight

Read 1 Corinthians 12:7–10. Ask the group how they see these gifts at work in the life of Christ (wisdom – paying taxes to Caesar;

knowledge – Gadarene demoniac; prophecy – prediction of Peter's denial; healing – Lazarus, the widow's son, Jairus's daughter).

Equipping for works of service

Read Ephesians 4:1–13. The Spirit equips us for the tasks of living with others and serving them. The five gifts described in verse 11 can be part of who we are in every sphere of life, not just when we gather with the church.

Lead the men in the prayer activity below to help you all grasp this further.

Pray

This small group can be part of your 'waiting in Jerusalem' pilgrimage. It helps you take time to reflect and become aware of the prompting of the Spirit regarding your future direction.

Ask the men to select one of the giftings below that they value and would like to see flourish in their lives:

- Vision and a pioneering attitude
- Communication and persuasiveness
- Compassion and practical care
- Understanding and wisdom
- Analysis and foresight

As each man shares his choice get the group to pray for the empowerment of the Spirit in that gifting. (This may be better carried out in smaller groups of three to four.)

These are the giftings of the apostle, the evangelist, the pastor, the teacher and the prophet (Ephesians 4:11). They help to build the kingdom of God in every context, not just in the institutional church.

2

Finding the Father

Men of the Spirit move from religion
to relationship.

'Wait for the gift my Father promised.' (Acts 1:4)

I have never liked my name. Presumably my parents thought that
Howard was a suitable name to give their son, and although it
wouldn't have been my first choice if I had been given a say in the
matter, it is, I suppose, reasonably acceptable. But why they then
decided to give me a second name, Edmond, my mother's maiden
name, I will never understand. The initials H.E.L. made school
life for me, the son of a clergyman, much more difficult than it
might otherwise have been.

Although I dislike my name, it is true to say that I dislike it less
than some of the names people call me. Howard is frequently
changed to Harold, while Joe, Sunny Jim and Blot on the land-
scape are often used as substitutes. There is, however, one name I
do enjoy being called – one name that always causes my heart to
thrill and never ceases to create a feeling of warm delight and
satisfaction within – and that is the name Dad. Even after 14 years
of parenthood, I still haven't lost the wonder of being a father.

There are many names given to God throughout the
Scriptures, but of all those names, perhaps none is as telling as
that of Father. It is unfortunate that because of the inevitable
imperfections of human fathers, so many of us fail to see the
glorious implications of that name when applied to God – implications of his involvement in our creation, his constant presence
with us, his unfailing awareness of our needs, his insatiable
appetite for our well-being, his sacrificial giving for our blessing,
his unimaginably rich and generous provision for our future.

God's choice of the name Father is the clearest possible statement of his longing for relationship with us. So many, inside as well as outside the church, have failed to grasp this. If asked to define Christianity, we so often resort to statements of doctrines that are to be believed, rituals that are to be engaged in and practices that are to be adopted or abstained from. In a word, 'religion'. But the essence of the gospel is an invitation to move away from religion and to enter into a living, vital, dynamic relationship with this Father God. Yes, doctrines, rituals and practices are important, but they are not the heart of Christian living. That heart is relationship. Living moment by moment, day by day with God.

How does that relationship come into being? It comes after we have waited in Jerusalem, after we have experienced the transforming power of the Spirit of God. He, and he alone, can bring us as children into the family of the Father God. There is, quite simply, no other way.

I have sometimes considered the question, 'Who was the most religious person ever to have lived?' Perhaps it was one of the great Old Testament characters like Adam, Abraham or David. Perhaps it was a New Testament personality – Mary or John the Baptist or the apostle Paul. Perhaps it was someone from church history like Augustine or Luther or Calvin, or perhaps a saint of later times like Billy Graham or John Stott. We will never know, because it is impossible to measure religious depth and fervour, but I want to suggest that one strong contestant for the title would have been Nicodemus. In terms of religious qualifications, knowledge and practice he had everything going for him.

Three things are said of him in John 3 that affirm his status as a man of deep religious standing. First, he is spoken of as a Pharisee, that group of misguided but well-meaning men who, coming from the lower middle classes, genuinely tried to make the law understood by and relevant to the needs of the common man. Their religious fervour was unquestioned. Hours of each day would be set aside for the study, learning, application and teaching of the Old Testament Scriptures.

Second, it is recorded that Nicodemus was a member of the

Jewish Ruling Council, the Sanhedrin, the chief court of the Jews to which only the most knowledgeable and respected men could be appointed.

And third, in addition to all of that, Jesus, during the course of his conversation with Nicodemus, described him as 'Israel's teacher'. Whether Jesus meant that Nicodemus held that role by right as a Pharisee and a member of the Council, or whether he was implying that Nicodemus personally was recognised as an expert, we do not know. But it matters little. He was the one to whom all matters of religion requiring a judgement could be brought, all questions on religion needing an answer could be presented, all issues of religion demanding a ruling could be set forth. In terms of religion, Nicodemus lacked nothing.

Even more striking was the contrast between Nicodemus and his fellow Pharisees. While they showed nothing but scorn and disdain for Jesus, he was much more sympathetic, recognising that there was something unique in Jesus, something of God in Jesus, and he expressed that recognition by his approach to Jesus at night, not for the purposes of confrontation and condemnation, of which his colleagues were so often guilty, but in order to discover more about this person who fascinated him to such an extent. If an awareness of Christ's godliness and an eagerness to listen to him can be described as religion, then this fourth qualification can, without question, be applied to Nicodemus.

Yet to this most religious of men came some of the most blunt words that Jesus ever spoke: 'No-one can enter the kingdom of God unless he is born of water and the Spirit' (John 3:5). The greatest mistake a person can make is to confuse religion with a relationship with the Father God that only the regenerating, birth-giving work of the Holy Spirit can accomplish in our lives, and which alone can make us right with God.

The Father we can find through relationship

If there is one word that summarises the fatherhood of God, that word is 'love'. Henry Blackaby writes:

God Himself pursues a love relationship with you. He is the one who takes the initiative to bring you into this kind of relationship. He created you for a love relationship with Himself. That is the very purpose of your life. This love relationship can and should be real and personal to you. (*Experiencing God*, Broadman & Holman, 1998)

But even that clear statement of the nature and purpose of God leaves us with a question: What does God's love look like when it is directed towards us? The answer is provided by Jesus, himself the supreme illustration of God's love, and also through his storytelling. Recorded in Luke 15 are three separate stories about love. Even Jesus, the master storyteller, found it impossible to capture in a single story the essence of the Father's love, so he told three stories, each one highlighting a different aspect of God's love. The context of these stories is the absolute misunderstanding on the part of the Pharisees and the teachers of the law as to why Jesus was mingling with the wrong sort of people: 'But the Pharisees and the teachers of the law muttered, "This man welcomes sinners and eats with them"' (Luke 15:2).

Jesus seizes the opportunity to describe the love within the Father heart of God. The first story relates to a lost sheep. The shepherd, aware of the sheep's awful vulnerability as it lies exposed to the cold of the night, goes in search of it. He knows that the missing sheep isn't experiencing the life that he wants it to have, but is trapped and limited in its existence. It is a statement of God's desire for us to experience the best possible life. In a day when so many have a mental picture of a God who is restrictive, limiting and joy-stealing, it is a necessary and timely reminder that love is exactly the opposite to that.

The second story, which tells of a lost coin, refers to the value God places upon us. As a widow, the woman in the story had no way of increasing the money she had on the day of her husband's death, and revolves around the fact that when she became a widow, she would have budgeted her money for the rest of her own life. To lose one coin was devastating, throwing her budget into total disarray and threatening to plunge her into life-threatening poverty. She placed such enormous value upon each of her coins that she turned her house upside down in her attempt to have it in her possession again. In a day when many people place such little value upon themselves, it is a reminder that no one is valueless to God.

The final story of the lost son tells of a boy who stole what did not legally belong to him. Wishing his father dead because he was a barrier between him and his inheritance, he impatiently and rebelliously demanded that inheritance immediately. To have then gone and wasted that inheritance only added to the boy's wickedness. His eventual, penitent return to the father, however, was marked not by accusations, judgement and punishment, but by total pardon and forgiveness. The Father's love, affirms Jesus, is a pardoning love for sinners. When so many today are paralysed by guilt and shame, the message of pardon needs to be clearly heard and understood. *Men of the Spirit find the Father who loves us passionately*.

The fear we must experience through relationship

While it is absolutely essential that we have a correct, life-changing understanding of the loving nature and purpose of the Father, it is equally essential that we never lose sight of the majesty, holiness and glory of God. The apostle Paul points out that we have received 'the Spirit of sonship' (Romans 8:15), but this should never allow us to lose a sense of awe and reverence in our relationship with God. Isaiah the prophet records in chapter 6 of his prophecy his own reaction and response to his awareness of the glory of God: 'Woe to me! . . . I am ruined! For I am a man of unclean lips, and I live among a people of unclean lips, and my eyes have seen the King, the Lord Almighty' (verse 5). Such a response of fear is inevitable when the Spirit reveals the Father to us. Where there is no fear, no overwhelming sense of sin and of utter unworthiness, there has been no real understanding of the nature of God. *Men of the Spirit fear God*.

The future we can anticipate through relationship

John has known a great deal of tragedy in his life. He has lost both a teenage son and a baby daughter. Yet there are few people I have met with a stronger Christian faith or a deeper certainty of reunion in heaven. Few of my friends have a clearer understanding of the nature of eternity and the meaning of death than he does. He speaks of life not as the few years we spend on earth, 'the here and now', but as our continual existence, 'the here and then', and he sees death as simply a small event during that ongoing life. For John, eternal life is lived now, not simply in the future. Henry Blackaby writes about the future in this way:

> God did not create you for time. He created you for eternity. Time (your lifetime on earth) provides the opportunity to get acquainted with Him. It is an opportunity for Him to develop your character in His likeness. Then eternity will have its fullest dimensions for you. If you just live for time (the here and now), you will miss the ultimate purpose of creation. Your life as a child of God ought to be shaped by the future (what you will be one day).

As religion gives way to a relationship that the Spirit of God makes possible for us, and we start to focus less on time, 'the here and now', and more on eternity, 'the here and then', two things begin to happen. First we begin to lose our fear of death and become excited about the future, and second we begin to order our lives in such a way that we invest our limited earthly time, energy, talents and resources in things that really matter rather than in treasures that moth and rust destroy and thieves steal. *Men of the Spirit focus on the future.*

The fellowship we can enjoy through relationship

'Fellowship' is perhaps one of the most over-used and misused words in our Christian vocabulary. On numerous occasions we are invited to enjoy a time of fellowship, when in reality what we are being invited to is simply an opportunity to share the same

geographical space with other Christians. While that is often the
essential context within which fellowship can take place, it is not
fellowship in any meaningful sense. Fellowship is not to be
defined as 'being in the same place', but as 'working together to
accomplish agreed tasks, to achieve agreed targets, to arrive at
agreed goals'.

Moving from religion to relationship brings us into fellowship at two levels. First it brings us into fellowship with one
another as Christians. Matthew 4 records the calling of the first
disciples, and speaks of how Jesus called Peter and Andrew to
follow him. We can only imagine the delight they felt as they set
off on their new life with Jesus. But that delight was to be short-
lived, for in a moment or two it would be replaced by horror as
Jesus stopped again and invited James and John to come along
as well. James and John were the competition, the opposition!
They were the people who fished just along the bay, and everything that went into their nets meant less for Peter and Andrew.
Here was intense rivalry, but an encounter with Jesus meant
that rivalry was set aside, and fellowship and partnership took
its place.

The second level of fellowship is more dramatic still. We are
called into fellowship not only with one another, but with God
himself. The very thought of this is staggering. The God who has
created everything that exists, voluntarily enters into a fellowship
relationship with me. It is the apostle Paul, writing to the
Corinthian church (1 Corinthians 3:16), who describes that fellowship most graphically: 'Don't you know that you yourselves
are God's temple, and that God's Spirit lives in you?'

So incredible is God's desire for relationship and fellowship
with us that he not only draws near to us, but he has chosen to
live within our individual lives by his Spirit, and having done so
he now invites us to respond to that by walking with him on a
moment-to-moment basis.

Many of us struggle with maintaining a vital and dynamic
devotional fellowship with God. Overwhelmed by the busyness
and demands of life, at home, in the workplace and often within

the local church as well, the first thing to go is time to be with God. Henry Blackaby writes about his own struggles to maintain meaningful fellowship with God:

> Early each day I have an appointment with God. I often wonder what happens when the Father who loves me comes to meet me there. How does He feel when He asks, 'Henry, where are you?' and I am just not there?

It has been a help to me to realise that to spend time each day with God is not a rigid requirement but the expression of a real relationship. If I approach fellowship with God from the standpoint of it being something I *must* do, it can so often become a matter of drudgery. But when I focus upon the fact of my relationship with God through grace, I find myself longing to arrange my timetable in such a way that there is sufficient time for those devotional practices that nurture my fellowship with God. *Men of the Spirit function through fellowship*.

The faith we must exercise through relationship

The reality of our relationship with God is proved or disproved by faith; by our willingness to give not just mental agreement to certain biblical statements about the nature and purposes of God, nor to give moral approval to certain accepted religious practices. Faith is our response to God. It is our understanding that what God says to us in Scripture is true, and our moving on from there to live in the light of that truth is essential in every area of life. Faith that does not produce a life of radical trust and unreserved obedience is not faith at all. It may have been written almost a century ago, but the old chorus that urges us to 'trust and obey, for there's no other way to be happy in Jesus but to trust and obey' is as urgent a message for the church today as it has ever been. Without trust and obedience, the twin elements of genuine faith, there is little evidence of a real relationship with the Lord.

It needs to be said as well, of course, that faith is not only absolutely necessary but extremely difficult at times. When we exercise faith, we are saying to God that we are setting aside our own agenda and becoming totally aligned to his. It is the difference between working *for* God and working *with* God. When we work *for* God, we set the agenda, we determine the limits to which we will go, we establish the method of working. We say to God that we would like to help him out and this is how we intend to do so. When we work *with* God, he sets the agenda, determines the limits and establishes the method, and invariably the work to which he calls us is much bigger than anything we would dare to take on through our own initiative. To work *with* God is a scary thing; a faith-demanding thing.

Think of Moses after he encountered God in the desert place as he was looking after his father-in-law's sheep. God demanded faith. God said to Moses, 'Go to Pharaoh,' while he was a fugitive from justice, having spent half a lifetime hiding from Pharaoh. God said to Moses, 'Tell Pharaoh to set my people free,' when those people were the workforce upon which the Egyptian kingdom depended. God said to Moses, 'Lead the people across the Red Sea,' when all Moses could see was a vast expanse of water. God said to Moses, 'Provide food and water for the wandering Israelites,' when Moses was surrounded by a wilderness and a rock.

Each of these challenges, and many more besides, were an invitation to Moses to work not *for* God but *with* God; to take on God-sized tasks, terrifying tasks, seemingly impossible tasks. Faith is more than belief. It is belief translated into radical action; belief expressed in trust and obedience. *Men of the Spirit follow in faith*.

The challenge we face is to abandon stationary Christian living and to move from religion to relationship. To walk with God, to find him as our Father, to fear him as a holy, awesome God, to live today with a confidence about tomorrow, to have fellowship with our brothers and sisters in Christ, and to exercise faith that demonstrates itself in absolute trust and unreserved obedience as we work with God for his glory. Such a move is beyond us if we attempt to make it in our own energy, but those of us who have waited in Jerusalem, and have become men of the Spirit, now possess the necessary resource. We have found the key to finding the Father.

SMALL GROUP STUDY

Discuss

Ask the group to tell of a positive memory of their friendship with their fathers, or to relate a positive memory of a special time with their own children.

Reflect

Ask the group to think of some of the key ordinary things Jesus did with his disciples, such as eating, fishing, beach barbecues, sleeping while they worked. Prompt them to think of Jesus' life as a carpenter/builder before his years of public ministry. (Key thought: relationship is found in the small things as well as the amazing incidents and special provision that God brings.)

Instruct

The chapter you have just read explores the three parables of 'lostness' that Jesus told. To help your men grasp something of the extent of God's love, you might like to do a reflective reading together of Luke 15:11–24.

Answer the following questions. Under each one is a short reflection to help you if the group don't have responses for all of them. The object of the exercise is to help us understand the emotional response of Jesus' listeners at the time and gain a deeper understanding of this important story.

- *What do you think the father might have felt when the son asked for his inheritance? (It was rare but not without precedent.)*
  Devastated? The raising of the money or the use of savings or the selling of livestock could have impacted the local economy and the lives of more than the immediate family.
- *When his money ran out, just how bad did the situation become?*
  The crowd listening to Jesus would have been shocked. Pigs were unclean animals to the Jews. It's a mark of how far the son had fallen.
- *What is the sign of the son's repentance and contrition?*
  His willingness to be a servant and to seek his father's forgiveness.
- *Does anything astonish you about verse 20? Read it again.*
  'While he was still a long way off' the father saw him and ran to him. It would have been seen as undignified for a man of the father's age to run, and with his clothing it wouldn't have been easy.
- *Would we feel compassion for someone who had effectively wished us dead?*
  Some commentators believe that the welcoming embrace and affection were to protect the son from locals enraged that he had returned. This makes the story all the more poignant.
- *How did the father demonstrate his love and forgiveness?*
  'So they began to celebrate.' The best food, the family heirloom ring, the robe reserved for mayors and civic leaders. The father's love was not mere words.

Respond to this story with the prayer activity below.

Pray

A helpful response to a reflection on the mercy and grace of our Father in heaven is to pray prayers of thankfulness and declaration. You might want to use the ACTS memory aid.

Adoration

Read or have someone read Psalm 103:1–12. Pray or invite your group to pray in response to the character of God revealed in these verses.

Confession

Spend a short time reflecting on the last few days. Ask God to forgive you for anything you've said or done that you now understand you shouldn't have.

Thanksgiving

Whether alone or in a group, thank God for specific blessings in your life. Thank him for the wonderful things you'll always remember, but also for the everyday blessings of food, family, friends and creation.

Supplication

Think about the week ahead. Do you have a major project, a specific time with family or friends, or the possibility of deepening a friendship with someone who doesn't know Jesus? Ask God to empower and equip you in all of these things.

3

Witnessing to the World

Men of the Spirit move from
secrecy to sharing.

'You will be my witnesses.' (Acts 1:8)

It had been a long and tiring day. My friend and I had sailed from
Northern Ireland to the Scottish port of Stranraer in the very
early hours of that day and had enjoyed the facilities on an
almost deserted ferry. Few others had felt the need to rise and
travel quite so early. Now at the end of a busy day at a confer-
ence centre in the north of England, we were returning home and
had arrived at the port with only minutes to spare before the mid-
night ferry back to Northern Ireland. On our approach to the
terminal I casually expressed the hope that the ferry would be as
quiet on this journey as it had been almost 20 hours earlier.

As we drove up the ramp onto the car deck it immediately
became obvious that my hopes would not be realised. The crew
directed us to one of the last remaining free spaces on the deck,
wedged in between coaches and minibuses, cars and motor bikes.
We were therefore expecting a crowd as we made our way up the
stairs towards the passenger lounge, but nothing prepared us for
what we were about to encounter.

There in the lounge were over 800 supporters of a well-known
Scottish football club, returning home, unhappily, from a match
that had been played earlier in the evening in which their team
had been totally outclassed and comprehensively beaten. It was
clear that most had turned to alcohol to drown their sorrows.

My reaction to the sight before us was to say, 'Oh no!' and to
seek out a quiet corner in which to bury my head in a magazine
for the next three hours. My friend, however, seeing the same

people in the same situation, said, 'Oh yes!' and set about the task of getting to know a group of these people, engaging them in conversation and presenting them with the gospel.

For my friend, evangelism comes naturally. Or does it? Perhaps it is more accurate to say that he finds evangelism a natural thing to do, because God has created within him an outgoing personality, God has presented him with many opportunities to share his faith with others, and God has given him the spiritual gift of evangelism – one of many spiritual gifts listed in the New Testament. But where does that leave me, and so many like me, who are 'Oh no!' people, whose God-given personalities are more shy and introverted, whose opportunities are more limited and whose spiritual gifts direct us to other areas of Christian service?

Does it give us the option of opting out of the evangelistic agenda of the church? Can we excuse ourselves from the Great Commission on the grounds that we are unsuited to the task? In Acts 1, Jesus makes no attempt to categorise his followers. He does not say to some that they are on the evangelism team that will in time change the world and to others that they are excluded. He calls all, he challenges all, he commissions all. But it is interesting and significant that Jesus, as he leaves his disciples, declares not that they will be 'evangelists' but that they will be 'witnesses'. Jesus recognises that even among the small group of believers to whom he gives the commission to go out and make disciples, there will be those who are evangelists, having the personality, opportunity and gift for that, and there will be those who are not evangelists for one reason or another. Evangelists and witnesses. There is a vital distinction between the two.

As with all spiritual gifts, the possession of the spiritual gift of evangelism is usually evidenced by effectiveness. God uses evangelists to bring people to faith on a regular basis.

What is a witness?

Peter gives one of the clearest answers to that question: 'But in your hearts set apart Christ as Lord. Always be prepared to give an answer to everyone who asks you to give the reason for the hope that you have' (1 Peter 3:15). Peter portrays a witness as a person with a two-directional relationship: a relationship with the Lord and a relationship with others. He speaks of being ready to explain our faith, to share our story of Jesus, to give an answer to the questions others put to us about our Christian hope. Now it is very unlikely that Peter had in mind, as he wrote these words, a scenario where total strangers will approach us and invite us to speak to them about spiritual issues. That doesn't happen today and it didn't happen in Peter's day either. Peter is thinking much more of the opportunities that will arise for us to speak about Jesus to those who know us well – our own family, those with whom we work, people we meet on a regular basis. A witness is someone who has meaningful relationships with other people.

But, says Peter, a witness is also someone with a vital and dynamic relationship with God; someone who has found the Father, someone whose life has been radically transformed by such an encounter. In fact, unless there is that radical transformation, unless Christ is Lord over our hearts, we will never have the opportunity to answer people's questions because those questions will never be put to us. The opportunity to share our story is the by-product of a radically transformed life.

I have no doubt that this is one of the most urgent issues we face within the Christian church today. Our witness and evangelism bear so little fruit. This is not because God has lost his power to save sinners, nor because the Holy Spirit has lost his ability to convict men and women of sin, nor because the edges of the sword of the Spirit which is the word of God have become blunted, but for the simple and fundamental reason that God's people have forgotten how to live. We have lost sight of what it means to be a radical follower of Jesus Christ, and our lives lack the spiritual integrity that is so essential if others are to notice us and want to know what makes us different.

It was a particularly cold and wet Sunday lunchtime as we returned home from church. Walking from the car towards the back door, we realised that there was something on the doorstep, which, on closer examination, turned out to be a tiny, new-born puppy. Probably no more than a few days old and separated from its mother, it was in a pathetic and critical condition, hours if not minutes away from death. Standing there looking at it, we held a family debate as to what should be done. One strongly expressed opinion was that we should do nothing at all, except ignore the dying animal and let nature take its inevitable course, while the majority opinion, expressed by those family members more caring and compassionate by nature, was that the pup should be brought into the warm while we made contact with the rescue centre and arranged for responsibility to be passed on to them. While that view won the day, it was made very clear that any hospitality offered was to be on a very temporary, short-term basis.

Having been brought into the house and fed a few drops of warm milk with a medicine dropper, the tiny creature began to show signs of revival and survival. To say that its health improved immediately and dramatically would be an exaggeration, but at least there were clear evidences that death was not inevitable. The animal began to demonstrate a strong constitution, a fighting spirit, and a liking for the attention being lavished upon it. It obviously had no intention whatever of giving up such privileges without a fight. Very soon, our offer of temporary shelter was replaced by the recognition that this was the start of a long-term relationship, a relationship which was to last for almost 17 years.

Realising that the pup had come to stay we were faced with the task of giving it a name, and this proved much more difficult than we had imagined. Rex, Rebel and Rover were quickly crossed off the list of possibilities, as was Sunday, in acknowledgement of the day on which the dog became a member of the family. After many frustrating attempts to find something appropriate, inspiration struck. The sermon that morning had been one of a series about the travels of the people of God from slavery in Egypt towards the freedom of the Promised Land, and had been dealing specifically with the occasion when the Israelites had come out of their tents one morning to discover a bread-like substance on the ground. Never having seen such a thing before they asked the obvious question: 'What is it?', or in their language 'Manna?' It was quickly agreed that Manna would be a great name for our new pet, as there was no evidence of it belonging to any particular breed that might be registered by the Kennel Club.

Over the years, Manna proved to be a wonderfully useful name, not least in the area of evangelism, for on numerous occasions it gave us the opportunity to share the gospel with others. When, from time to time, we had to report to the local police station because of some misdemeanour on the part of the dog, we would be asked the dog's name, and almost always an expression of surprise and puzzlement would appear on the officer's face, along with a request to explain such an unusual name. I have often thought that the evangelistic conversations that followed did more to increase the numbers of the Christian Police Association than any other single element. Often, in the local park, other dog owners would engage us in conversation, and inevitably the name of one another's pets would be asked. Again, Manna needed an explanation and provided an opportunity to share the gospel. We had so many evangelistic opportunities during Manna's long life that we celebrated his tenth birthday by changing his name to Billy Graham!

Manna, 'What is it?', is a great name for a mongrel dog, but is it appropriate for a child of God? Perhaps it is. In church we profess and appear to be followers of Jesus, and yet throughout the rest of our week we live lives that are little different from those around us. People justifiably think, 'I hear what you say about your Christian faith, but when I see how you relate to your family, how you treat other people, how you drive your car, how you complete your tax return, how you are as materialistic as your next door neighbour, how you are dishonest in your business dealings, I have to ask what you really are.'

The urgent need is not for more seminars about evangelism, more books on evangelism, more projects for evangelism; the greatest and most urgent need is for us as Christian people to remember how we are supposed to live, to begin living holy, godly, radically transformed lives – lives under the control of the Spirit of God and under the authority of the word of God. When this relationship is right, then our relationship with others will lead to the opportunity to share our Christian faith.

What is a witness? A person with a relationship with God that is lived out within the context of their relationship with others.

Effective witness

Even in our increasingly secular and godless society, people are still coming to faith, and research reveals that the single greatest influence upon people is relationship with others. While we have a vast range of excellent evangelistic programmes and numerous resources that explain the Christian faith and encourage people to embrace that faith for themselves, it is still the case that people are impacted more by other people than they ever are by pro-grammes and resources.

What are the necessary elements within such a relationship if it is to be used by God to bring people to faith?

Genuine friendship

If those people into whose lives we enter sense that our motives are simply to see them converted to Christ, they will very soon raise the defences and become hardened towards the gospel. What is required on our part is a willingness to be a friend for friendship's sake alone. Certainly we will want to see our friends come to faith, and we will pray for them and speak to them when the opportunities to do so sensitively present themselves, but we are to make a friendship commitment to them, regardless of the eventual spiritual fruitfulness of that friendship. Nor is this something short-term. We are to commit ourselves to long-term, life-long friendship. I well remember hosting a visiting speaker who one evening during his stay in our home received a phone call from his wife, informing him that a friend had been converted earlier that evening. My guest reported this piece of news to me with the comment, 'I have given that man one day of my week for the past 42 years.' In fact I think he was a little hurt that after such a commitment of time and friendship this man should have come to faith when he was not present!

A servant-like attitude

There is a need for us to demonstrate that we have no personal motive or agenda other than that of being a servant to those whom we befriend. In a society where, it seems, everyone is prepared to use others for their own purposes, a genuine servant heart is a powerful testimony to a life that has been transformed. I was recently caught up in a lengthy traffic jam, stopped immediately behind a bus. On the back of the bus was an advertisement for a very well-known national store that proudly announced 'More than 30 years serving the community'. As I sat and reflected upon that claim, I couldn't help but feel a little sceptical. I wondered whether, if the profits had not reached expectations, the firm would have remained in our locality for those 30 or more years. In reality what should have been written on the back of that bus was 'More than 30 years serving ourselves'. And, of course, in business that is perfectly permissible. The creation of wealth demands profit-making. But we who are witnesses to Jesus need to be able to say with integrity, 'We are serving the community.' We have no other motive, no other concern, no other agenda than to promote the good of those whom we serve.

A balanced and approachable personality

There are two extremes we need to avoid as we build witnessing relationships with others. First is the extreme of being so exceptionally pious that our friends conclude that we are living on an altogether different planet from the one they inhabit. We can give the impression of being so untouched by the common struggles, pressures and failures of this world that our friends sense we would not understand their problems and so they hold back from discussing spiritual matters with us.

The second extreme is that of being so worldly that our friends say to themselves that if Christianity makes so little difference to us, there is little point in even considering it as an option for their lives. They are looking for something more radical than we demonstrate. Both of these extremes erect barriers to witness. A few years ago a friend took me to a McDonald's restaurant located immediately beside the Tower of London. I know nothing about the history of the building where the restaurant is housed, but I was immediately struck by how well it fitted into its environment. It was designed in the same style and built of the same stone as the surrounding historic buildings and it blended in perfectly with its environment. Yet at the same time, on the front of the building, was the huge yellow 'M' that identified it, unmistakably, as a McDonald's. As I saw that building I realised that here was an illustration of the type of people we need to be if we are to be effective witnesses: real, normal, approachable people who easily and naturally blend in with others, yet at the same time are distinct from others and clearly identifiable as people of God. This balance is not always easy to maintain, but it is a powerful element in our witness when, with the power of the Spirit, we demonstrate it in our lives.

An ability to share our story intelligibly

On a recent flight I was mystified by the conversation going on around me. In the window seat of the plane was one of the country's leading engineering experts, while in the aisle seat sat a post-graduate research student. For the duration of the flight they discussed concepts and projects that were meaningless to me as I sat between them. Although they were both speaking English, I had as little understanding of what they were talking about as I would have done if they had been speaking Swahili! Their language was specialised.

Those of us who spend much of our time within the Christian community easily forget how foreign our language and thought processes are to those who are outside the church, and we underestimate perhaps the difficulty our friends have in understanding the gospel. Biblical words and concepts that are totally familiar to us can be like a foreign language to them. An important part of effective witness is learning to put ourselves in the shoes of the unchurched and to communicate in a language that makes sense to them. Let me tell you a story that illustrates this.

'Have you ever been saved?' he asked me as he blocked my way to the front door of the store.

'Pardon?' I replied.

'Saved,' he repeated. 'Have you ever been saved?'

'Well yes, I suppose I have,' I answered. 'There was one time when I was swimming in Spain and I got out of my depth and . . .'

'No,' he interrupted, 'not that. You know, *saved, really saved*, redeemed, born again, washed in the blood. You know what I mean.' I didn't know at all what he meant. 'Look,' he said, 'read this.' He thrust a little booklet into my hand. On it was a picture of hell with the words 'Good News' written in large letters. 'I hope this will lead to you being convicted.'

'Now wait a minute,' I protested. 'I may occasionally drive a little faster than I should, and I have once or twice parked on double yellow lines, but I'm sure I'm not guilty of anything that might be serious enough to get me convicted.'

'You really don't understand, do you?' he asked in what was by now an exasperated tone of voice. 'Listen,' he said, 'perhaps we could meet next week when you've had time to read the booklet, and we can discuss things over a cup of coffee.'

With some reluctance on my part, we agreed to meet on the following Thursday. When the day arrived, he apologised for being late for our appointment. 'Sorry,' he exclaimed breathlessly, 'I was having my quiet time and was transported into the heavenly kingdom.'

'Quiet time! What do you mean?' I asked innocently.

'Well, every day I study the word and pray in my closet.'

'Your closet? You pray in a closet at work?'

'No, not at work,' he retorted. 'In my car.'

'You have a closet in your car?'

He changed the subject.

As we talked over the little booklet he had given me the previous week, I saw that I needed to be saved, redeemed and born again, so I committed my life to Jesus Christ. My new friend was overjoyed.

'What you need to do now,' he advised, 'is to find a good body.'

I must say that I was a little surprised at his suggestion, but it sounded good to me, so I took his advice and set off at once for the local health club in search of an attractive lady. When I met Joanne I knew at once that I had met the right person for me, and when she too became a Christian shortly afterwards, we planned to marry.

We enjoyed being part of a lively local church together, but I still had a lot to learn. One Sunday I wasn't well and couldn't get to the services. My friend met me the next day and said, 'Wow, you really missed something special yesterday. God moved in a big way.'

I was devastated. 'Moved? And just when I was getting to know him. Where has he moved to anyway?' I asked.

'No,' said my friend. 'He hasn't moved away. It's just that people were really set on fire for him yesterday.'

I don't know what it is, but sometimes this fellow and I seem to have some difficulty communicating with one another.

It's been two years now since I was saved, redeemed and born again. I'm committed to a good body, God keeps moving and I'm on fire. But I have one ongoing problem. It seems that all my old friends just don't seem to understand me any more. When I tell them that I've been washed as white as snow, they look really puzzled. Perhaps they're just convicted.

The tool for witness

As we have already seen in 1 Peter, it is necessary for every believer to 'be prepared to give an answer to everyone who asks you to give the reason for the hope that you have'. Those who possess the spiritual gift of evangelism may well feel able to give such an answer in terms of a formal presentation of the gospel, but those who lack that gift and who would classify themselves as 'Oh no' people may well struggle at this point. But evangelists and witnesses alike share a powerful evangelistic tool: their own individual story of the work of God in their lives. This story, or testimony as many call it, has incredible potential. Our unsaved friends may well argue with us over a huge variety of doctrinal issues, but the one thing with which they cannot argue is our story – a story of what Jesus has done and continues to do in our lives. The supreme example of a personal story in Scripture is that of the apostle Paul, recorded for us in Acts 22.

What we learn from this biblical example is that there are three distinct parts to our story. We need to share the story of what we were like before we became a Christian. Paul does that in verses 2–5. The second part of our story tells of the circumstances through which we became a Christian, which Paul does in verses 6–13. The final and essential part (verses 14–21) is the sharing of what Jesus means to us today and every day.

Those with whom we share our story may well find our pre-conversion life interesting, but it is unlikely that their story and ours will coincide completely. We may have had a Christian upbringing, for example, while they may have come from a totally unchurched background. We may have been absolute rebels, while they were paragons of virtue. Nor may they be able to identify with the circumstances through which we came to faith. I have a friend who was converted on a flight from Bangkok to London. As his plane dropped almost 20,000 feet during a violent thunderstorm, he very definitely (and very wisely) committed himself to the Lord. Few of our friends will ever find themselves in that situation. But the third part of our story, what Jesus means to us today, is the one thing with which all our friends will be able to identify. What they really want to know is whether committing their lives to Jesus Christ will make a difference. Whether it will help them lose a burden of guilt and shame about past sin, whether it will give them a sense of meaning and purpose in what is now a meaningless and directionless life, whether it will help them cope in times of heart-breaking crisis, whether it will remove their crippling fear of death and the future. Our story answers that question.

Realising that our story has these three parts is also a great help to those who don't know the exact moment or place of their conversion. They so often feel that their story is not worth telling because there is no dramatic moment or event to share with their hearers. By making their story the story of today, a today infused with Jesus, they have the potential to communicate a life-changing message to their friends.

In Romans 5:8 Paul deals with the mind-blowing fact that 'while we were still sinners, Christ died for us'. Our inevitable response to that, argues Paul in verse 11, is that we will 'rejoice in God through our Lord Jesus Christ, through whom we have now received reconciliation'. The word translated as 'rejoice' is an interesting one. It is found nowhere else in Scripture. It literally means 'to go about boasting'. The apostle's argument here is that, as those who have moved from religion to relationship, we will feel compelled to move also from silence to sharing. We will actively look for and seize every available opportunity to let others know what has happened in our lives.

As with the other changes that are necessary in our lives, this is not something we can do by ourselves. To attempt to do it through our own resources is to condemn ourselves to failure and to stationary Christian living. Sharing takes place only when we become men of the Spirit and learn to depend entirely upon the power of God through the work of his Holy Spirit to equip us for the exciting task of witnessing to Jesus.

SMALL GROUP STUDY

Discuss

Describe a memorable day in your life other than your conversion or your wedding day (if either of these apply). Who were you with? What made it so memorable?

Reflect

Make a list of all the incidents you can remember in Jesus' life that involved him eating, or talking about eating.

Instruct

Read Luke 10:5–9. A fourfold pattern emerges:

The declaration of peace (verse 5)

This has several layers of meaning. It suggests acceptance and goodwill towards those you are meeting. Are there evangelism methods that undermine this idea?

Eating together (verse 7)

This reinforces the sense of acceptance and mutual respect. Jesus often showed his love for broken humanity by eating with those whom others shunned.

Discuss together what happens alongside the simple act of eating when people have a meal with each other.

Praying for need (verse 9)

Read the verse again. Should people wanting healing and prayer be committed Christians?

Declaring the kingdom

After the acceptance, fellowship and prayer, Jesus instructs them to share their faith and point to him.

This key 'sending out' passage may challenge our understanding, as we normally practise the reverse of the above process.

Pray

Pray for people from each of the groups below, who are not followers of Jesus. Take one group at a time and have the men share briefly about someone they would like to pray for. Encourage them to pray for specifics up to and including coming to faith.

Family

This will usually include the extended family of cousins, aunts, uncles and so on.

Friends

These are people you might be in a club or society with, or have known for many years.

Workplace

We spend a lot of time at work and have many different levels of relationship. Pray that trust will grow in these relationships.

Neighbourhood

Your neighbourhood acquaintances might include the milkman, the postman, the people at the shops. Pray that your snippets of conversation will be a foundation for a growing friendship.

4

Encountering the Enemy

Men of the Spirit move from
comfort to commitment.

'You will be my witnesses in Jerusalem,
and in all Judea and Samaria,
and to the ends of the earth.' (Acts 1:8)

The results of the personality type test were interesting and
revealing. For the first time in our marriage, we understood why
we see things so differently, not least in the context of our annual
holiday plans. We discovered that one of us has a personality that
works best in a structured environment, and needs things to be
planned in a careful and detailed manner, while the other enjoys
an unstructured approach and is more comfortable behaving in
a totally spontaneous way. That explains a lot. We share a
common passion for caravanning, so each year harmony reigns
until the moment when the caravan is hitched to the back of the
family car and we head for the ferry. Then it ends! The planner
in the family won't allow us to drive onto the ferry until we know
the exact details of where we are going, when we will get there,
where we will stop on the way, and how long we will stay when
we arrive. Although I have never served in the armed forces, I
imagine that less planning went into some of the major military
campaigns in our country's history than goes into our family hol-
idays. The spontaneous member of the family would much
prefer to leave the ferry port and follow the road that has least
traffic on it at that moment. Where we eventually arrive is a
matter of little concern, and having arrived there spontaneity
demands that our stay is short before we take to the road again,
any road again, in search of some new, unspecified destination.

We are given little indication in Scripture as to the personality types of the early disciples, but we can be quite sure that the travelling Jesus speaks about in Acts 1 is not because they were all spontaneous people, dissatisfied with any one place after a short period of time. In moving from Jerusalem to Judea, from Judea to Samaria, from Samaria to the ends of the earth, they were not satisfying some deep-seated wanderlust. Rather, Jesus is speaking here about persecution, about opposition, about encountering the enemy. He was telling them that their lives from this moment on would be lives of pain and sacrifice; lives where nowhere would be a safe refuge from the attacks of Satan and from the consequent opposition. And so it proved to be. 'On that day [the day of Stephen's martyrdom] a great persecution broke out against the church at Jerusalem, and all except the apostles were scattered throughout Judea and Samaria' (Acts 8:1).

The reality of warfare

It is easy to be critical of one another in our day and to say that we have lost the realism of the inevitable opposition to the people of God, but clearly it was something that even the early church struggled to grasp. Both Peter and John felt it necessary to speak plainly on the issue, in remarkably similar terms. 'Dear friends,' wrote Peter, 'do not be surprised at the painful trial you are suffering, as though something strange were happening to you' (1 Peter 4:12). And John wrote, 'Do not be surprised, my brothers, if the world hates you' (1 John 3:13).

Yet it needs to be admitted, doesn't it, that all too often we are surprised. Despite all we read in Scripture about taking up our cross and following Jesus, all we sing about being wholly available to him regardless of the consequences, all we know about the Lord's return to vindicate his people and his cause, and all we believe about heaven being the place of ultimate and final reward, we still insist on the right to a quiet, peaceful, unopposed life as Christian men, and we are devastated when we face the first sign of rejection or opposition. We need, as a matter of extreme urgency, to hear Jesus say again, 'You will be my witnesses in Jerusalem, and in all Judea and Samaria, and to the ends of the earth.' There will be no permanent resting place for us here on earth, because our lives will be lived in constant warfare with the enemy.

The reason for warfare

My son developed an interest in cars and in all things to do with them at a very early age. On one occasion, when he was about three years old, we were driving along a road and he commented critically on a car coming towards us with its headlights on even though it was a bright summer afternoon. As the car drew nearer he corrected himself saying, 'Oh, it's a Volvo. It can't help it.' Volvos, as you may know, can't help it! They are wired in such a way that the headlights illuminate at all times.

In the same way, Satan can't help being evil all the time. Jesus speaks clearly of Satan as a fallen angel: 'He was a murderer from the beginning, not holding to the truth, for there is no truth in him. When he lies, he speaks his native language, for he is a liar and the father of lies' (John 8:44).

In the Old Testament, Isaiah records Satan's initial proud rejection of God's purposes, and his insistence upon his right to equality with God:

> You said in your heart, 'I will ascend to heaven; I will raise my throne above the stars of God; I will sit enthroned on the mount of assembly, on the utmost heights of the sacred mountain. I will ascend above the tops of the clouds; I will make myself like the Most High.' (Isaiah 14:13–14)

His nature and personality as a fallen angel lead him inevitably and invariably into opposition to God, and therefore the same grace that brings us peace with God brings us warfare with Satan. The moment God created the world and viewed it with deep satisfaction, seeing its perfection as a reflection of his own, Satan came and destroyed that perfection. When God instituted family life as the first principle for human existence (Genesis 2:18) Satan came and tore husband and wife apart, causing Adam and Eve to blame each other for the act of sin and rebellion. When God established the commandments with Moses, Satan came and declared that man should live as he pleases, and prompted us to live without restraint. When Jesus came into the world on his divine mission to save sinners, Satan took him to a wilderness and tempted him to settle for something less. And now, when men and women exercise saving faith and experience peace with God, becoming members of God's family and builders of God's kingdom, Satan opposes them. He can't help it. It is his nature: fallen, corrupt and wicked, and opposed to God and everything about God and everyone who loves God.

The nature of warfare

We have seen already that the Holy Spirit exercises three distinct but interrelated ministries within our lives. He empowers us for service as we depend upon him, he brings us into a vital relationship with God, and he uses us as men of integrity to be witnesses to Jesus Christ. It is precisely in these three areas that Satan attacks us. His enmity against God is an enmity directed against the work of God in our lives.

First, Satan attempts to make my Christian service ineffective

He knows well the struggle I have with the concept of depending upon God, and he is constantly coming and assuring me that I don't need God any more for effective service. He sends me to Scripture to prepare for preaching and he tells me to get on with the task. He assures me that I know my way around the Bible well enough, and I understand it well enough not to need to spend time in prayerful preparation as I once did. Satan doesn't mind at all how much I read the Bible, as long as I do so without a sense of dependence upon God.

He sends me up the pulpit steps on a Sunday morning, convinced that I am a good orator and have enough charisma to be able to carry the people with me – so much so that the Holy Spirit is not at my side as I go up those steps. Satan doesn't mind if I preach with passion, as long as I do so without dependence upon God.

He sends me to visit the sick, or attend the church leadership meeting, or teach the Sunday school, or lead in the youth club, or drive the church bus, happy for me to be engaged in any or all of these things, or any number of other service opportunities, as long as I do so without dependence upon God. He cares little about how busy I am, even in Christian activity, as long as I am busily engaged in the energy of my own resourcefulness.

As well as attacking me through all these internal struggles, from time to time Satan finds those who will attack me from the outside. Those who will stand against me, those who will oppose me, those who will criticise me, those who will denounce me. And although the people who encourage and support me far outnumber those who criticise and condemn me, I am so easily defeated by discouragement. Internally and externally Satan is on the attack, attempting to make my service ineffective.

Second, Satan attempts to immerse me again in religion rather than relationship

He draws me away from relationship with God by constantly presenting to me the sins and failings of the past and by haunting me with the thought of them. He makes me doubt that God's grace could possibly be big enough to sweep away my deserved condemnation, and he forces me to live a depressed, defeated life.

He draws me away from relationship with God by blinding me to the intensity of the love of God for me. He convinces me that God's love is like my own – fickle and conditional.

He draws me away from relationship with God by sometimes going to the other extreme of making me so aware of my forgiven condition that I lose all sense of being a debtor to grace, and I take God for granted. All reverence and awe and godly fear disappear.

He draws me away from relationship with God by making me

uncertain about the future. He convinces me that this life is all there is to human existence, so that I live in dread of death, regarding it as the ultimate defeat of all my plans, the dashing of all my hopes and the shattering of all my dreams.

He draws me away from relationship with God by bringing such pain to my body and fear to my mind that they form a dark cloud, blotting out the sunshine of God's presence with and purpose for me.

He draws me away from relationship with God by making me proud and arrogant, telling me that I do not need the help and support of others in my Christian living, and he makes me cold and compassionless, unwilling to offer help and support to my fellow believers. He makes me again what I once was – an isolationist – because he knows that it is much easier for him to defeat me when I reject rather than rejoice in fellowship.

He draws me away from relationship with God by robbing me of my faith, so that while as a Christian I do not doubt God's word for a moment, I refuse to launch out into the deep water of trust and abandonment, and remain ineffective in the shallow waters of the harbour of known experiences.

If, as Satan attacks me, he is trying to make me abandon religion, he fails on every occasion. I have never rebelled against religion. But I don't believe for a moment that he is concerned about religion. He has a much more sinister agenda. He tries to make me abandon relationship with God. He allows me to continue with my religious living, for it poses no threat to him, but he tempts me to make that living a substitute for a meaningful relationship with God. Even Satan recognises that ultimately, because of grace, that relationship can never be broken, but he recognises too that he can totally rob me of the joy of that relationship. And so often that is exactly what he manages to do.

Third, Satan veils my witness to Jesus Christ

If, as we have said, the key element of such witness is a life of integrity, Satan finds it horrifyingly easy to lead me along a road of non-integrity. In my words, my actions, my ambitions, my relationships, my attitudes, my lifestyle, there is so often such an utter lack of holiness that the image of Jesus is obliterated from my life. All that is left is my verbal profession of faith and story of conversion, but that counts for nothing, coming as it does from someone whose life cries out that Jesus does not really reign over it.

Victory in warfare

How do we handle such enmity? Is constant defeat inevitable? Are we doomed to be failures as Christian men, living stagnant, ineffective Christian lives because of Satan's opposition, or at best experiencing the limited growth and maturity that Satan allows? Of course not. Scripture is absolutely clear that victory is both possible and expected.

> Therefore put on the full armour of God, so that when the day of evil comes, you may be able to stand your ground, and after you have done everything, to stand. (Ephesians 6:13)

This verse makes two things very clear. First, God has provided sufficient armour for us to gain victory over every attack and temptation that Satan brings into our experience. To abandon hope, to give up the struggle, to stop resisting the evil one, to lose sight of the glorious possibility of victory, is to deny both the power and the provision of God and to elevate the power of Satan to far too high a position.

And, second, the armour we have is from God. It is not the plans that *we* draw up, the resources that *we* manufacture, the determination that *we* exhibit which will give us victory and help us to move forward towards maturity; it is what God, by his Spirit, does in our defence that succeeds.

What is this armour of God? Paul describes it as something made up of six separate elements.

• *The belt of truth* is that absolute conviction we can have of the truth of the gospel. Jesus, when faced with the temptation to abandon his eternal ministry in favour of short-term benefits, again and again resorted to the same defensive weapon, countering successive temptations with the words 'It is written'. He knew the truth; he wore the belt.

- *The breastplate of righteousness* is the confidence we can possess that the obedience and sufferings of Jesus have totally satisfied God, and that they have been credited to our account, bringing us out of the enemy's kingdom and eternally into the kingdom of God.

- *The readiness that comes from the gospel of peace* is the high spiritual morale that comes from knowing we have peace with God.

- *The shield of faith* is the ability to protect our minds from the unholy, evil, proud thoughts with which Satan would fill them. It is putting into disciplined practice Paul's exhortation, 'Whatever is true, whatever is noble, whatever is right, whatever is pure, whatever is lovely, whatever is admirable – if anything is excellent or praiseworthy – think about such things' (Philippians 4:8). When our minds are filled with good things, there is little room left for Satan to insert those thoughts that will pollute our minds.

- *The helmet of salvation* is the wonderful realisation that although spiritual battles still rage, the decisive battle has already been fought and the ultimate victory has been achieved.

- *The sword of the Spirit, which is the word of God*, is perhaps the foundational weapon. The psalmist wrote about it in Psalm 119:11: 'I have hidden your word in my heart that I might not sin against you.' He was not thinking of hiding in the traditional sense of the word. Married as I am to someone who has never lost her childlike excitement about Christmas and birthdays, I have regularly found it necessary, having bought a present to mark the occasion, to hide it somewhere to prevent her from finding it before the appropriate day. Recently I did such a good job of hiding it that even I could not find it when the day arrived, and I suffered the abusive accusations of having forgotten to buy her a present. The psalmist is thinking of hiding the word in an altogether different way. He draws his illustration from the world of cooking. Just as salt is often applied to food in the preparation stage, and disappears, becoming absorbed into the food, so the word of God is to be absorbed into our hearts, the control centre of our lives. Though the salt is invisible, the difference it makes to the taste and wholesomeness of food is remarkable, and in the same way the word of God, hidden or absorbed within us, affects everything we say, do and think.

The sword of the Spirit, along with the other God-given weapons, when used aright, guarantees an effective defence against the enemy we encounter on a daily basis. Those weapons are communicated by the Spirit of God to those who are men of the Spirit, and lead away from ineffectual Christian living to a life of maturity and triumph over the enemy.

SMALL GROUP STUDY

Discuss

This chapter refers to the value of 'hiding God's word' in your heart. Is there a Bible verse or passage that has been a source of inspiration or comfort to you at a specific time or throughout your life? Explain why.

Reflect

Jesus could have changed the world on his own, but he is relationship orientated because of his fellowship within the Trinity with the Father and the Spirit. He modelled relationship and dependence on each other while he was on the earth.

Ask the group who Jesus' closest friend was on earth. (John.) Who were his other close friends? (Peter and James.)

We can't be best friends with everyone. The group you are in is the 'Twelve' for your men. Encourage them to think about being in a prayer triplet (a 'Three' group), and to ask the Lord for a long-term ('One') friendship. (If they're married they have this already, but a male friend they really trust is a vital aspect of their overall friendship spectrum.)

Instruct

What happens when we hide the word of God in our heart? It equips us to defend ourselves against Satan's accusation, but it also enables us to undermine his activity in others.

Read Proverbs 10:21. Ask the group to share encouragements they have received over the years – nourishment from the mouths of others.

Read Isaiah 50:4. The NIV translation speaks of 'an instructed tongue' that knows 'the word that sustains the weary'. Ask the group if they have had any experiences of sharing a scripture with someone as part of their encouragement to them during difficult times.

Pray

This is a simple but powerful way to reinforce experiences the group have had of sharing scriptures with others.

Ask the men to write down the reference of a verse they have shared with someone in the past and to give it to someone else in the group. Explain that as you pray together each man should read out the verse they have been given, as they feel prompted. The person whose verse it was can then pray in response, thanking God for his provision in the past, and requesting his wisdom for the future.

Postscript

One of the most humbling experiences of my life has been to get to know Ivan, a Bulgarian Baptist pastor, who ministered during the most dark, difficult and dangerous days of the Communist regime in the Soviet Union. He has told me often of the many years of imprisonment he experienced for the 'crime' of preaching about Jesus. The conditions he endured were horrific in the extreme. Incarcerated for twenty-three-and-a-half hours of each day, despised and abused by his fellow prisoners because of his faith, cut off from any contact with his wife and children, and subjected to outrageous and inhumane physical suffering, he prayed each day for freedom. His story is amazing because there was not a single day during his imprisonment when he was not offered the opportunity of freedom. All that was asked of him in exchange for release was to sign a declaration that he would no longer promote his Christian beliefs. Despite his torment within his prison cell, each day the offer was rejected with the statement that while he loathed prison, he loved Jesus more. I asked him on one occasion how he had had the strength to resist the temptation of giving in. His answer was one word: '*Borga*' ('God').

He is a man who has waited in Jerusalem. Having been energised by the indwelling power of the Spirit of God, he can never be satisfied with a life of mere activity. He longs for accomplishment. He is a man who has said 'no' to religion but the loudest possible 'yes' to a relationship with God. He is a man who has refused the option of silence and committed himself to sharing.

He is a man who has rejected comfort and embraced commitment, despite the terrible cost. He is a man who has had enough of spiritual ring roads and is determined to move forward. He is a man of the Spirit.

May we be like him.

Howard Lewis

Key Principles for Small Group Study

There must be dozens of books available on small group work. You may want to explore some of them as your group develops. In this short guide, however, we want to outline some of the keys to an effective men's small group.

Venue

If at all possible, meet somewhere informal with comfortable chairs. It makes a difference to people's perception. Talking with friends evokes a warmer response emotionally than rattling around inside a church hall.

Food

Think about the following: Jesus' first miracle of changing the water into wine, the feeding of the five thousand, Jesus' visit to Zacchaeus's house, the Last Supper, the meal in Emmaus, the first thing Jesus did for his disciples following his resurrection, Peter's vision on the rooftop, the parable of the banquet and the parable of the prodigal son. World-changing events happening around meal tables! Perhaps if your community activities could happen around a meal table they would go on to change the world! There is a different dynamic when people eat together than when they simply gather.

Group size

To enable most of your group to respond to the discussion questions, you may like to break into twos or threes for each question and then gather the whole group together again for the reflection and instruction. The twos and threes may also be useful for the prayer times.

Use of 'we' and 'you'

If you are doing the instruction, try to say 'we' rather than 'you' when talking about the issues people face and potential responses. Otherwise it could suggest that you consider yourself to be a saint and everyone else to be a sinner! Identifying with the group by using 'we' suggests that you are neither arrogant nor lacking in sympathy for other people's situations.

Delegation

This resource book seeks to recognise that people are often 'passion' rich but 'time' poor when it comes to serving Jesus. The clear outlines here mean that the leader of the study can set aside time to be familiar with the leader's material but be confident that all the other aspects of the meeting are already to hand. This in turn means that those who don't feel that they are preachers or teachers can still guide their friends through the study. Some will discover confidence in the safe environment of a group of friends.

Dissent

It has to be a key value of your group that you will agree to disagree agreeably. When you don't concur on an issue, the object of the exercise is not to 'win' but to clearly state your position and let others reflect in the coming days and weeks on what has been said.

You will want to preserve Christian orthodoxy as the foundation of your group, but also to practise 'principled tolerance'. You are not searching for a way of reconciling everyone's views. You are simply saying that you can't compromise on the person and work of Christ, but you're not going to allow division to creep in over different views of, for example, the end times.

Your men will often have tough questions they never dared ask lest they be viewed as unspiritual. They need to feel safe to explore those things among friends.

Dealing with the dominant

There are some who will speak about everything and constantly interject into the conversation. This can slowly kill a group, turning it into a negative experience. In the most extreme cases you may need to be blunt with such people, but do it in private before you ever do it in public.

If you read the seven letters to the churches in Revelation chapters 2 and 3, you will note that the Lord commends them all before rebuking five of them. There is a vital wisdom here. Use affirmation before you steer the group back on course. Agree with something the dominant person has said and then refer the discussion back to the person they interrupted. By doing this, you signal to the group that the discussion won't be controlled by one person's opinion, while at the same time stopping someone without shaming them.

Of course the dominant person could be you! Try to steer the discussion by asking open questions – even when you already know the answer. You can still get people to your teaching goal without simply telling them everything.

50 Outlines for Men's Meetings

by Howard Lewis and Dave Roberts

The church has long understood the benefit of
gathering men together in small groups. Jesus gathered
his disciples in this way. John Wesley proved the value
of allowing men to help and challenge one another.
Today is no different.

The 50 outlines in this book will allow men to discover
principles that will help shape their character in the
following areas:

- their relationship with God
- home and family
- the workplace
- the wider community
- church

A focused approach to conversational learning will
enable men to share stories of faith, reflect on Scripture,
receive instruction and pray together.

GREAT IDEAS